THE BOOK of MARVELOUS CATS

Janet Kozachek

ISBN: 978-0-578-18191-2 (sc)
ISBN: 978-1-4834-5564-8 (e)

Because of the dynamic nature of the Internet, any web addresses or links contained in this book may have changed
since publication and may no longer be valid. The views expressed in this work are solely those of the author and do
not necessarily reflect the views of the publisher, and the publisher hereby disclaims any responsibility for them.

Janet Lynne Kozachek

Lulu Publishing Services rev. date: 8/12/2016

Acknowledgments

I would like to thank the following persons for their support and contributions to The Book of Marvelous Cats; my husband, Professor Nathaniel Wallace, for his enthusiasm and encouragement, my sister, Jessie Thompson, for compiling the first one-of-a-kind hand-bound book of these illustrated rhymes for the cat, and my friend, Kristina Miller, for her continued review, contributions of photographs and graphic design. Much appreciation is due to my feline models, which include Kristina Miller's cats Bewie, Jag, Mickey, and Sadie as well as my late cat Max who was the consummate poser.

Preface

The Book of Marvelous Cats began as a Christmas gift from my sister. She gave me one of her hand crafted books. During a protracted illness I filled in the blank pages with fanciful images of imaginary cats. The cats did all the things I could not do at the time. They climbed onto rooftops to fix things. They tilled up the gardens. They did all the housework. One even removed tiresome guests that stayed too long from off of the premises. When the small volume was filled, I wrote rhymes to accompany the illustrations.

Shortly thereafter I reconnected with an old friend from my teen years who was an avid collector of Siamese cats as well as books about cats. I shared my small volume of illustrated rhymes with her and was inspired to create more of them. I wrote a second group of rhymes based upon our correspondence over the next two years and illustrated those with much larger and more elaborate drawings. Over time the book grew. The cats took on even more anthropomorphous and autobiographical qualities. They became idiosyncratic, often straying from the original theme of "usefulness." The later illustrations often incorporated images of earlier cats within the composition, in an ekphrastic picture within a picture motif.

Declaring the project complete, I added two last illustrations and rhymes to create a context for the work. These were the initial "Sleeping Kitty," and the ultimate "Kitty Awakens," setting the text as an unconscious fantasy awakening to the possibilities of the written word.

Table of Contents

Sleeping Kitty

Sleeping Kitty dreams of cats
wonderful, awesome, marvelous cats
Cats that serve us and cats to serve
Felines full of vim and verve
He dreams of the one who was his mother
cats of the world and many others

Acrobatic Cats

Acrobatic Cats do stunts
walking on fore paws with puffs and grunts
twisting and turning as they fly through the air
There is nothing that they won't do for a dare

Magic Cat

Magic Cat has many tricks
that he does for money or just for kicks
should his conjuring cause guests to fear
then Magic Cat will disappear

Pirate Cat

Pirate Cat wears a patch on his eye
while swilling a beer and eating fish fry
He hoists up the jib boom and fixes the rig
Then swinging to starboard he dances a jig

Designer Cats

Whether its checkerboard, stripe or polka dot
Designer Cats fit in any spot
You can have crazy quilts and a vase that's Ming
Designer Cats go with anything
So dress and decorate with flair
Designer Cats fit in anywhere

The Cat of Mardi Gras

She dons a pretty maiden's face
and wears pearls upon her paws
Her tail she waves in flawless grace
The Cat of Mardi Gras

Party Cat

Party Cat can sing and dance
In every country - even France
When you have friends to entertain
A festive aura he'll maintain

Yakkity Cat

Yakkity Cat talks all day long
(even though she knows it's wrong)
across a fence or on a phone
while driving a car or sitting at home

Bouncer Cat

When A guest becomes a boor
Then Bouncer Cat shows him the door
Your home will never host a slob
When Bouncer Cat is on the job

Guardian Cat

Across the valley from the top of the hill
Guardian Cat sits on his vigil
To protect the homestead on him we rely
Guardian Cat keeps all under his watchful eye

Garden Cat

Set him loose in your back yard
And Garden Cat works long and hard
Raking, weeding, seeding, feeding
Your old bones won't take the beating

Little Black Cat in a Garden

Crouching under hanging fruit
Little Black Cat sits small and mute
He does not long for company
and need not have your sympathy

Carpenter Cat

Carpenter Cat is not afraid of the roof
He climbs up tall ladders and down again as proof
With a hammer in his satchel and nails in his smile
He'll fix your whole house but it may take a while

Culinary Cat

Culinary Cat makes tuna fondue
that he cooks up for a party of two
with Kitty cream puffs and mouse pepper cheese
served up with lizard sauce - as much as you please
He never cooks anything straight from a can
Not even for his delectable mew goo guy pan

Mechanical Cats

Mechanical Cats do all the chores
They clean the oven and mop the floors
They roast the chickens and grate the cheese
And just about everything as you please

Massage Cat

Whether your sport is football or dressage
Your aching muscles will need a massage
Massage cat does as he is bidden
While carefully keeping his sharp claws hidden

Solar Cats

Solar Cats lie in the bright sunlight
on top of the roof in rows neat and tight
They come into the house when the sun goes down
Providing much needed warmth all year round

Lover Cat

Lover Cat wears a contented smile
He's been with his favorite puss for a while
Cavorting among flowers in the month of May
and in a room to themselves at their country chalet

Mommy Cat

Mommy Cat let out a purr
When kittens nestled in her fur
How sweet it is to remember then
When you were eleven, nine or ten

Vintage Cat

A Vintage Cat likes old styles
heirloom gardens and cobblestone miles
He sits in a wagon - a rustic antique
hand wrought from iron, oak wood and teak

Cargo Cats

Cargo Cats go along for a ride
even with no place to hide
They sit pretty still, they're not too heavy
and fit very nicely in a '57 Chevy

Little White Cat up a Tree

Little White Cat up high in a tree
Are you chasing a squirrel, or hiding from me?
You always run away when I come near
Is it from anger or is it from fear?

Dissociation Cat

Is he a tabby or calico?
Dissociation Cat does not know
Into altered states he takes a dive
where he has six toes and sometimes five
His tails go this way his arms go that
He cannot say where he is at.
He may have four claws or only three
and thinks a fly looks like a tree

Shaman Cat

Forget about your exercise
Shaman Cat will exorcize
your evil spirits and bad blood
They'll leave your body with a thud
Shaman Cat can see your aura
and change its color with fauna and flora
And he can fix a broken bone
just by warming up a stone
He'll cure the swelling in your eye socket
with magnets from his mystery pocket
He'll place kitty moss between your toes
and blow healing crystals out his nose
Shaman Cat knows that pussy willow
will help you sleep well upon your pillow
He'll clean your liver and kidneys too
and make sure you don't catch cat scratch flu
Do you believe all this is true?
If you do then Shaman you

Cave Cats

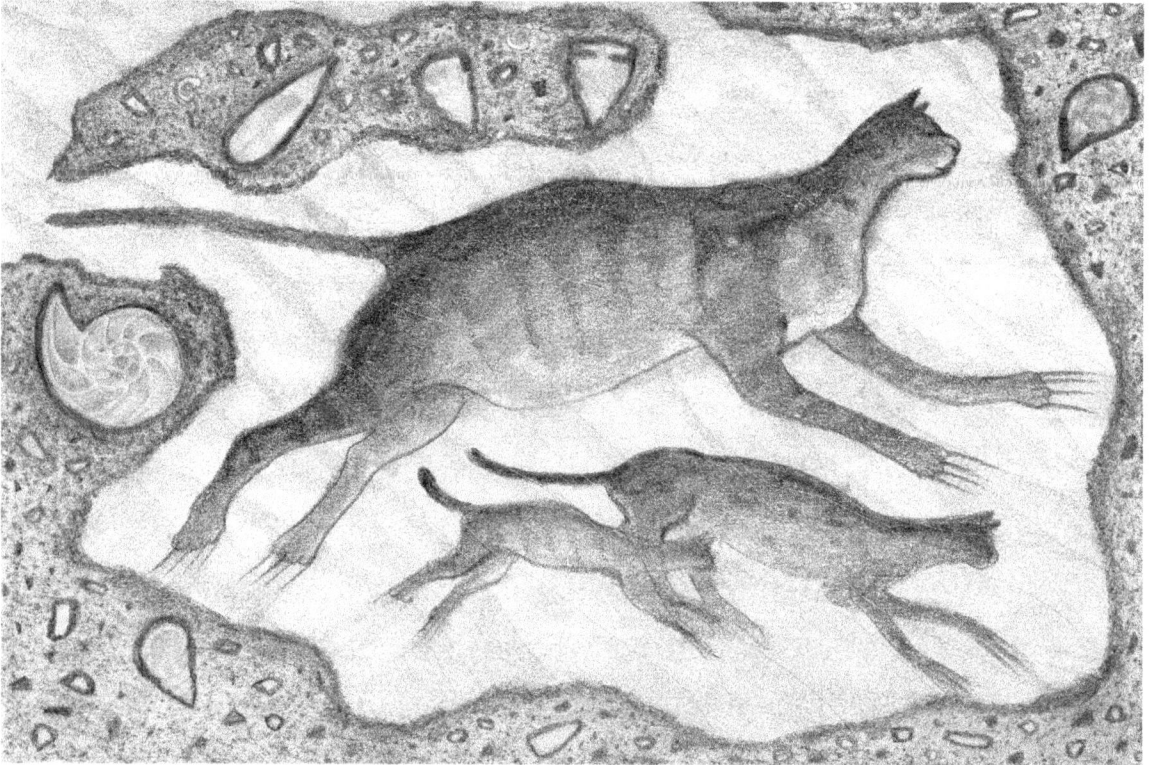

Cave Cats race across a wall
Unafraid to slip or fall
Their visages mysterious and mythic
Cave Cats enjoy being paleolithic

Aboriginal Cats

Aboriginal Cats have spots
and not just a few but lots and lots
Some jump, some play, others just mew
and one can play the didgeridoo

Abby Sinian

On an ancient carpet stands a marble cat
Abby was his name, his owner gave him that
Mr. Sinian, Abby Sinian loved to hunt and fish
Immortality in stone, he surely got his wish

Tomb Cats

In sacred spaces where spirits loom
Flying cats protect a tomb
Filled with objects for veneration
From ages past to the present generation

Cosmic Cat

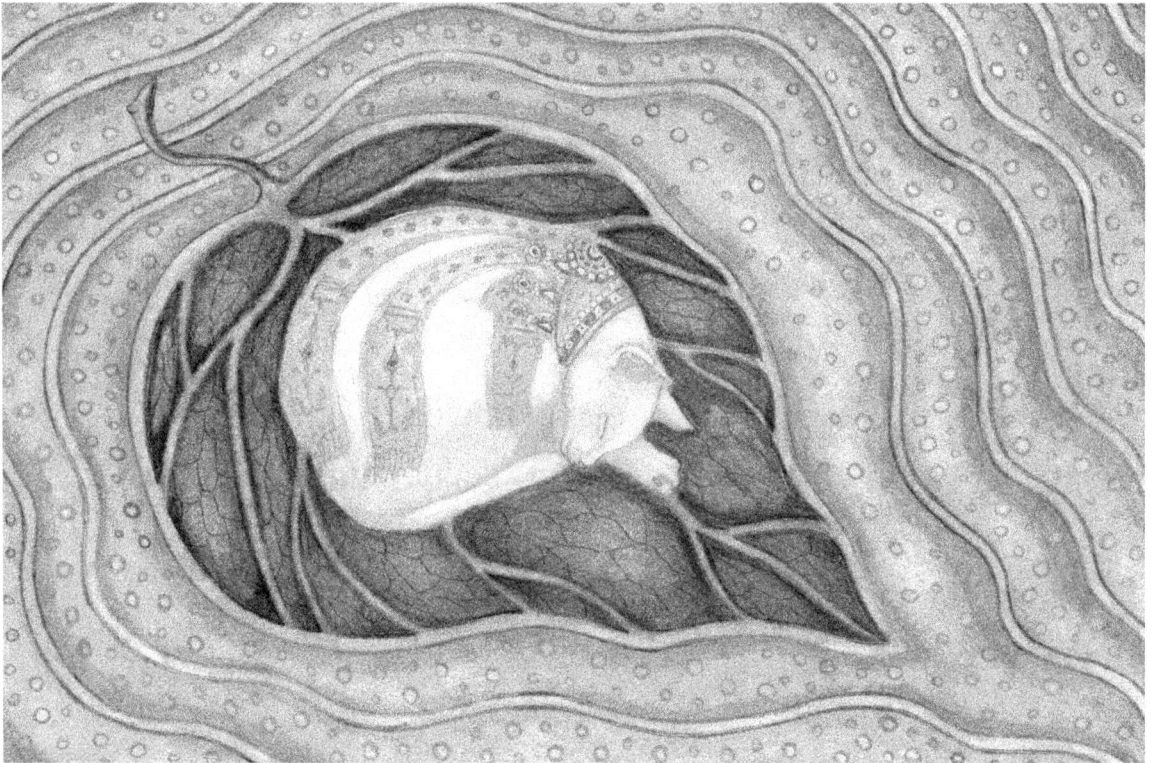

Cosmic Cat floats on a leaf in the sea
oblivious to you and to me
From worldly cares he is set free
and one with the universe he will be

Royal Cat

Royal Cat is the Queen's first pet.
Whatever Royal Cat wants, Royal Cat will get
The Queen tells all the other cats to leave him alone
Whenever he rests upon Her Majesty's throne
Royal Cat is allowed to do anything he pleases
This does not sit well with the Queen's Siameses
They claw threads out of her robe in less than a minute
Then hide to make it look like Royal Cat did it

Magnificat

I believe in one cat
In one cat, I believe
Magnificat, magnificat
My love he does receive

There is a Cat Like That

Kitty awakes to a beautiful day
Thinking of cats that sit, work, or play
They do wondrous things then strike a pose
There are many marvelous cats like those
Can he conjure a kitten from out of a hat?
There is indeed a black cat like that
Cleaning around the house with a buzz
There is one cat or another that does
He takes a pest out like one would a rat
There is a cat that works like that
Tiny ones that like to hide
There may be one or two inside
A Cat that cooks a sumptuous feast
There is such a feline beast
Ancient Cats carved into stone
and kittens only just half grown
A Cat that talks and a cat that sings
There are cats that do these things
You find them in the world and in a book
All you have to do is look

The End

www.ingramcontent.com/pod-product-compliance
Lightning Source LLC
Chambersburg PA
CBHW081239090426
42738CB00016B/3347